THE VISIONARY SHEEPDOG

THE VISIONARY SHEEPDOG

A Leadership Book

Susan J. Lindahl
&
Paul A. Lindahl Jr.

iUniverse, Inc.
Bloomington

The Visionary Sheepdog
A Leadership Book

Copyright © 2012 by Susan J. Lindahl & Paul A. Lindahl Jr.

All rights reserved. No part of this book may be used or reproduced by any means, graphic, electronic, or mechanical, including photocopying, recording, taping or by any information storage retrieval system without the written permission of the publisher except in the case of brief quotations embodied in critical articles and reviews.

iUniverse books may be ordered through booksellers or by contacting:

iUniverse
1663 Liberty Drive
Bloomington, IN 47403
www.iuniverse.com
1-800-Authors (1-800-288-4677)

Because of the dynamic nature of the Internet, any web addresses or links contained in this book may have changed since publication and may no longer be valid. The views expressed in this work are solely those of the author and do not necessarily reflect the views of the publisher, and the publisher hereby disclaims any responsibility for them.

Any people depicted in stock imagery provided by Thinkstock are models, and such images are being used for illustrative purposes only.
Certain stock imagery © Thinkstock.

ISBN: 978-1-4759-5523-1 (sc)
ISBN: 978-1-4759-5524-8 (ebk)

Library of Congress Control Number: 2012919313

Printed in the United States of America

iUniverse rev. date: 10/15/2012

CONTENTS

Introduction 1

Lesson in Leadership 2
Translating the Analogy 20
Understanding True North 21
Picking the Team 27
Understanding the Gaps 29
Defining "Critical Mass" 30
Planning to Get There 32
Learning and Translating "the Story" 34
Leadership Context 36
Facilitating Conversations 37
Setting the Compass 39
Providing That Compass 43
Sheepdogs Don't Rest Much 45

Conceptual Grounding 47
Reading List 49
About the Authors 51

To Nels and Jenifer for their encouragement to share this story and for their own demonstrations of courage and leadership. Parenting may be the ultimate leadership frontier.

To Thomas P. Kroehle, a truly gifted leader who, by Paul's great fortune, was demonstrating the message in this book as Paul learned it in his master's thesis project.

To Superintendent Joseph S. Hickey for charting "true north" for our family and fellow educators, and to Peggy Rose Hickey for modeling the moral center every day of her life.

And lastly, to the four-legged compass-keepers in our family—Max, Peppercorn, and Joey—and those that came before them . . .

INTRODUCTION

The following story is an analogy, or perhaps a business fable, constructed to put in perspective the role of a leader (who may be an executive) in an organizational intervention. The analogy is not perfect, but it may be of value in understanding the dilemma of the leader as organizational coach.

The idea was conceived and developed as part of Paul's master's thesis in an executive MBA program. The sleeping sheepdog was awakened during Susan's PhD research on leadership.

LESSON IN LEADERSHIP

This analogy illustrates a lesson in leadership that remains elusive to many.

Picture a fairly large island.

From only one point, on the very tip of the island, you can just barely see the mainland.

There is a group of people who have ended up wandering around the island and have no idea where they are.

On the island, there are enough tools, materials, and even books on boatbuilding and sailing to build a boat and sail to the mainland.

There isn't enough food to last long.

You are the only one on the island who knows where the mainland is and that everything is there on the island to build a boat and get everyone safely to the mainland.

The challenge is that you are a sheepdog.

Since you need to be the leader, you must be a very bright and *visionary* sheepdog.

But you are a sheepdog, and you can't tell anyone what to do.

So you do what a sheepdog does.

You start with one or two people and try to herd them. You herd them to the places where the tools, materials, and books are, and you hope they will pick those things up and begin to learn.

If you are lucky, some of the people are already carrying tools or books they've found, so you start with them.

If you are really lucky, some of them might even know something about boatbuilding or sailing.

You keep herding the people into more people and past more tools, materials, and books, circling around and around to keep the stragglers in the group.

Since you are a very visionary sheepdog, you know that sooner or later, these people are going to start talking to each other.

You know that as soon as you have enough of them, and they have enough of the tools, materials, and knowledge . . .

... they are going to figure out that they can build a boat and sail it.

Now, if they do that when they're on the wrong part of the island, they will have achieved a process of boatbuilding and sailing, but you could all end up anywhere ...

As a visionary sheepdog, you know that if you plan your herding well enough, you can have that critical mass of people, tools, materials, and knowledge come together at that one point on the island where the goal is clearly in sight.

Then what does the process become, and whose process will it be?

A remaining but important question for the visionary sheepdog is whether, after all the herding around, they will take you with them.

If you are a very good and visionary sheepdog, they will hardly even notice you are there.

The end . . . or better yet, a new beginning.

TRANSLATING THE ANALOGY

Putting the sheepdog to work begins with the following steps:

- Understanding True North
- Picking the Team
- Understanding the Gaps
- Defining "Critical Mass"
- Planning to Get There
- Learning and Translating "the Story"

UNDERSTANDING TRUE NORTH

Getting to the one point on the island . . .

What is "true north"?

Just as with a compass, what the instrument (or facts) seem to show may not be the whole story.

The needle on a compass points to the magnetic North Pole, which isn't located at the same point as the geographic North Pole. The geographic North Pole is on the axis the earth rotates around. The geographic pole is used on maps. The difference is the origin of the expression "true north."

The offset between magnetic north and true north is a variable that our ancestors learned the hard way some time ago. Navigators use reference values to correct to true north based on facts about where they are on the earth. It is still more interesting to note that the magnetic pole moves around over the years, so the correction for one point in time is not the same as for another. Just as with organizations, "true north" is literally a moving target.

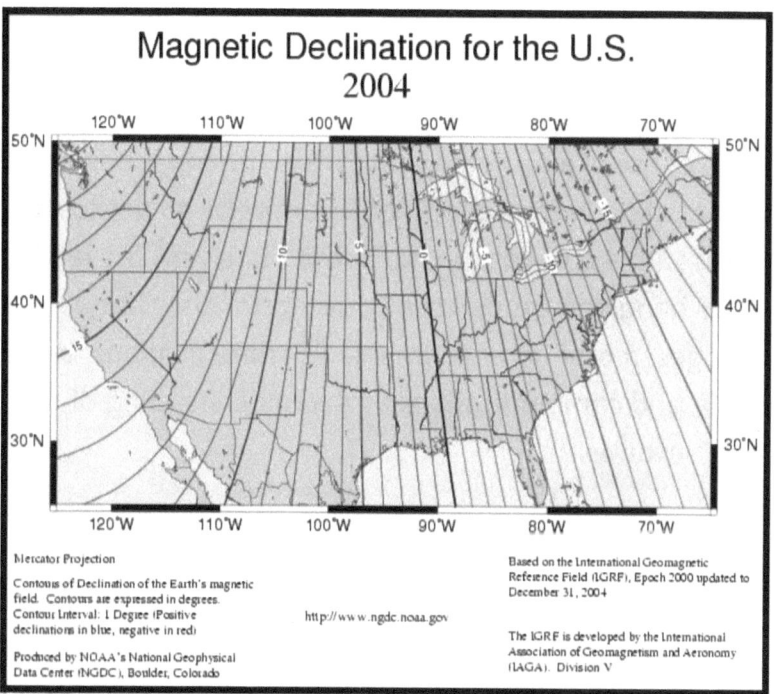

True north is not a destination; it's a frame of reference that enables use of a compass with a map. The correction must be based on time-appropriate information to get to true north with a compass. In much the same way, the leader must bring the group to a "true north" that frequently changes, requiring adjustments to strategic plans, team goals, and communications as the understanding of true north evolves.

In the analogy, a "true north" piece of information known only by the sheepdog is that there is a point on the island where the desired destination can be seen.

For a leader, it is important, before starting with the team, to find as many of such pieces of information as possible.

Examples might be the following:

- approaches to processes
- goal elaboration/definition of criteria for a goal
- mission/vision/values-driven criteria, such as greater good for the community in the big-picture perspective

Getting to the "true north" frame of reference is a journey that is ongoing. New information affecting the goal or approaches to the goal are likely to be discovered in the "herding" and team processes. The leader must be aware of the learning taking place by the team and must be prepared not only to learn and adapt, but also to herd toward the true-north-based goal.

"True north" is what the leader knows about getting to the goal and what the goal should include. It is analogous to being on the one point of the island where the mainland can be seen.

PICKING THE TEAM

Who do you herd?

Team members are key influencers and holders of key knowledge or skills, whether the scope of the team is big or small.

Team composition is a significant-enough subject to have been the basis of multiple books. Some factors for the context of this work are as follows:

- Homogenous groups may quickly become stale or dysfunctional.
- Whether you utilize the Myers-Briggs Type Indicator or other personality sorting, a constructive mix of types is a valuable organizational tool for the leader.
- The smaller the team and the more high-performance-oriented, the more significant the mix and balance of types becomes, as well as the composite personality type of the team as a whole.

The size of the team depends on what the team needs to accomplish (goals) and the time frame required. Stakeholders may be needed based on organizational entities as well as institutional or cultural constituencies.

UNDERSTANDING THE GAPS

Where do you herd them?

Identify information and skill gaps, by person and by group.

Plan how to facilitate the team's exposure to key information and skills.

Identify internal or external borders that may exist or emerge as issues, and have plans to herd through or around those borders toward the goal. Gatekeepers may become obstacles for navigation around, over, or through to the destination needed.

DEFINING "CRITICAL MASS"

When are you "there"?

When key skills and knowledge to ensure developing and completing the process have been acquired by enough of the group to recognize they can accomplish the goal together, critical mass has been reached.

The key factor for the leader is to guide the team so that understanding and visibility of "true north" influenced goals comes together as critical mass is reached.

Use tools to measure progress, such as key performance indicator (KPI) development and measurement and self-development actions (SDA).

Getting there requires "the map"—a full understanding of what is needed to describe and accomplish goals.

Making "true north" a part of bringing the goal clearly in sight involves, among the other factors noted, a conceptual synergy of mission, vision, and values. Understanding the need to model values for the group is a core responsibility of the leader in this context.

Getting to the "true north" frame of reference is something the leader must learn along the way, herding the team back away from distractions, when appropriate, and toward the goal. The leader must be sufficiently connected to the process to be able to see that critical mass is reached within clear sight of the goal.

PLANNING TO GET THERE

Are there stragglers, and can they be herded back into the group?

There may be stragglers and those who diverge from the team. A leader works to herd them back toward the goal.

Sometimes team membership must be adapted to accomplish the goals, particularly for a fast, focused, high-performance team.

One job of a team leader is to recognize when team members are either not contributing or are dysfunctional. To do that successfully, the leader needs not only a grounding in personality types but also a grasp of team dynamics.

All of that is necessary, along with the skill to observe team behavior effectively and influence or "herd" without dominating team activities.

The sheepdog analogy works here too, as survival and success factors are a part of the choices made.

No leader is 100 percent able to plan the process, so flexibility to adapt as you learn your team's capabilities is crucial to successful outcomes.

LEARNING AND TRANSLATING "THE STORY"

How to get to where the goal is visible at the right time.

The leader must learn how to articulate the organizational vision or "story."

With people it is more than just visual; the articulation of the story can be built toward the critical "goal in sight" moment.

Group learning builds more than individual skills; it also enables evolution of a common language around objectives, a common understanding of the compass tools.

The leader reinforces progress toward the destination while empowering team members to embrace the goal when they are ready.

This is adaptive learning both for the team and the leader.

LEADERSHIP CONTEXT

Peter Senge's book, "The Fifth Discipline; The art and practice of the learning organization" gives this paraphrase of Lao-Tzu, a Chinese philosopher from thousands of years ago: "The good leader is he [she] who the people praise. The great leader is he [she] who the people say 'we did it ourselves.'"

Most significant for leaders to learn is the role of relating the contextual story, as it differs from storytelling. It involves getting to the true "sight of the mainland" for the organization.

FACILITATING CONVERSATIONS

Facilitating conversations for your organization requires the courage to ask key questions:

What are the true prevailing issues?
Where do you need to go?
What will it take to begin the journey?

✗ Planning
✗ Mapping
✗ Direction

Invite, encourage, and reward differing opinions.

Do you have the courage to listen and keep people listening to each other, to sustain the dialogue just long enough for your organization to find the answers? This requires courage to begin... and *more* courage to sustain the journey.

It is likely that discoveries will be made along the way. Navigation is needed to go around or through them, using the compass tools but reinforcing true north. Courage is also needed to learn, adapt, and move forward, crossing borders where needed and encouraging border-crossing by others.

How do you navigate?

SETTING THE COMPASS

Top-down change may produce immediate changes in behavior. It is not likely to produce desired changes in the culture of the team or organization. It will not produce empowerment or that sense of ownership by the team that leads to truly motivated engagement.

A key part of leadership is providing the organizational compass. What is the compass? The compass helps the team to identify

+ direction
+ map
+ barriers and course corrections
+ "true north"

The team must keep the overarching goals in sight. The compass and map help the team maintain focus on the urgency and clarity of purpose.

The compass must exemplify moral courage and include shared values that relate to the "true north" frame of reference for your team or organization.

Keep in mind that it is not just about the ultimate destination; there are likely to be stops along the way. Side tours may not be welcome, but they are always opportunities to learn for visionary sheepdogs.

Magnetic north and true north vary by just a few degrees, but can get one very lost even with a map. Similarly, the "true north" frame of reference for organizations can mean the difference between success, failure, or mediocrity—or failure to survive for the long term.

PROVIDING THAT COMPASS

A key part of leadership is providing that compass. But how?

It's more than delegation. Focus on facilitating meaningful and courageous discussions. Focus on enabling the team; be a servant-leader. The right balance of skills and personality types within the team matters. Team members need access and encouragement to acquire needed skills for engagement of meaningful and effective processes and systems. The leader must model the mission, vision, and values before the team can embrace them, including the modeling of balance in life. Respect for the importance of family and community helps to keep the greater good in perspective as the story is told.

Civic engagement for a leader is a critical part of authenticity to tell the story.

Remember the importance of timing in order to reach critical mass with clear goals in focus.

When teams come to critical mass (the ability to act as needed) without shared understanding of the desired common goals, the outcomes are difficult to predict and will likely be unsatisfactory.

SHEEPDOGS DON'T REST MUCH

You may wonder whether our working sheepdogs get any rest. Right: they don't rest much while working.

But they know the difference between work and not-work.

They are also border-crossers. For human leaders, this occurs with people, organizations, and landscapes.

Leadership thrives on living a balanced life. It is a source of the moral compass or true north vs. the compass alone.

We invite you to share the journey. Enjoy!

CONCEPTUAL GROUNDING

Theorists
- Senge: learning organizations, the heart of continuous improvement
- Demming: Fourteen principles of continuous improvement and many others; continuous improvement in business organizations
- Boyer, many others: continuous improvement in educational organizations
- Birnbaum: border-crossing
- Greenleaf: servant leadership
- Kouzes and Posner: five practices; model the way, inspire a shared vision, challenge the process, enable others to act, and encourage the heart
- Myers and Briggs: personality type and influences on group behavior
- Lindahl: civic engagement as an enabler for breaking down the disconnect between individuals and the community

READING LIST

- Birnbaum, Robert. 2000. *Management Fads in Higher Education: Where They Come From, What They Do, Why They Fail.* San Francisco: Jossey-Bass.
- Boyer, Ernest. 1996. "The Scholarship of Engagement." *Journal of Public Service and Outreach* 1(1): 9-20.
- Demming, W. Edwards. 1986. *Out of the Crisis.* Cambridge, MA: MIT Press.
- Greenleaf, Robert K. 1996. *On Becoming a Servant Leader.* San Francisco: Jossey-Bass.
- Kroeger, Otto, Janet M. Thuesen, and Hile Rutledge. 2009. *Type Talk at Work: How the 16 Personality Types Determine Your Success on the Job.* Oakland, CA: Tilden Press.
- Kouzes, James M., and Barry Z. Posner. 2007. *The Leadership Challenge: How to Get Extraordinary Things Done in Organizations.* 4th ed. San Francisco: Jossey-Bass.

- Lindahl, Nels. 2006. *Graduation with Civic Honors: Unlock the Power of Community Opportunity*. Bloomington, IN: iUniverse.
- Senge, Peter M. 1990. *The Fifth Discipline: The Art and Practice of the Learning Organization*. New York: Doubleday.

ABOUT THE AUTHORS

Experience
- ✘ Susan Hickey Lindahl, MS Counseling Psychology, PhD Leadership; Paul A. Lindahl, Jr., BS Nuclear Engineering, Executive Fellows MBA
- ✘ more than thirty years each, one in education and law, the other as a recognized international leader in an industry spanning power generation and other diverse segments
- ✘ successful navigation by each of multiple profound organizational changes
- ✘ consulting for board-level leadership teams
- ✘ civic leadership and engagement
- ✘ passionate about family and our roles as grandparents for Katherine Marie and John Paul, golf, open waters, and coffee
- ✘ education is a family value; PhD, MBA, JD, PhD
- ✘ "She who listens with her eyes"—Choctaw/Irish INFJ—and "He who can't not lead" (per Myers-Briggs speak)—Swedish navigator ENTJ

www.ingramcontent.com/pod-product-compliance
Lightning Source LLC
Chambersburg PA
CBHW021038180526
45163CB00005B/2186